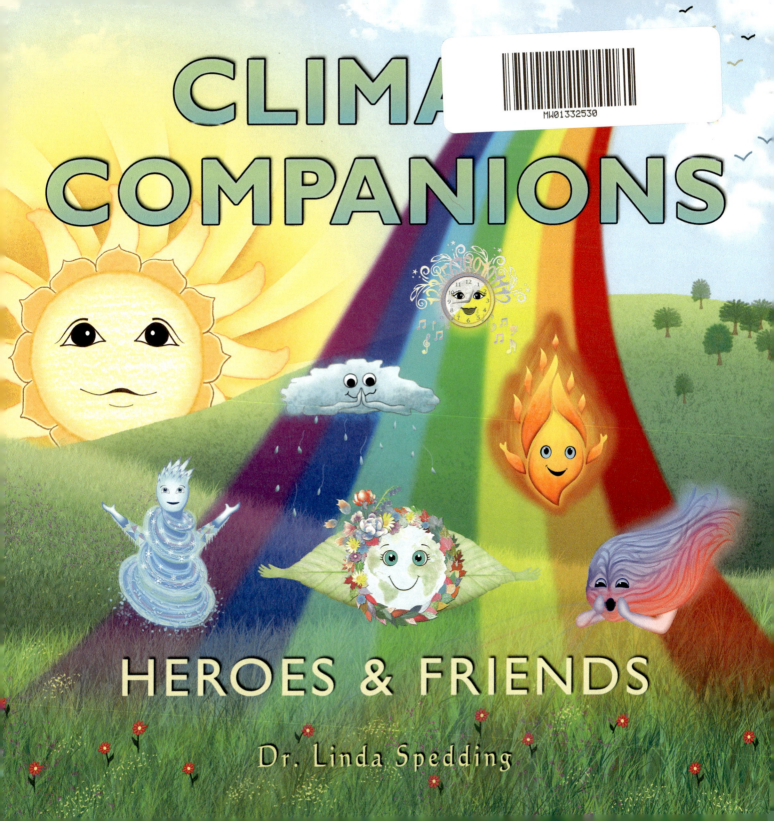
CLIMATE COMPANIONS

HEROES & FRIENDS

Dr. Linda Spedding

Copyright © 2015 Dr. Linda Spedding
All rights reserved
www.lindaspedding.org

Published by Purna Elements
www.purnaelements.org

Supporting the humanitarian mission of Dr. Svami Purna
Adhyatmik Foundation
www.adhyatmik.org

ISBN: 978-0-9891286-6-7

eeniemeeniebeeniebo.org

Dedication

To my son Ajan, to children everywhere and
to the Eternal Child in all of us,
and to my father who has recently departed

Acknowledgments

I wish to acknowledge Andreina Imery for the illustrations and publication design. I would also like to acknowledge Kaley Scarfato, my family and friends for their continued creative support.

It is my intention that these ongoing stories
will enable the reader to better understand
their relationship to Mother Earth.

Words from the Author

Wherever we live, a key question is "what is the weather like today?" The weather impacts us and we impact the weather. The weather affects our spirit, our mood and our day or days! We know that weather predictions and the climate in which we live touches our lives from daily food and nourishment to our ongoing health and happiness. Yet often we understand little about the way the elements work and any understanding comes from information taught and found by others. As an international environmental lawyer, adviser and writer I am so pleased to find a way to reach our young ones and their families and friends to identify more with the world of the weather and its wondrous ways.

With Climate Companions the intention is to empathise with and relate to the weather, to enjoy the variations and to take responsibility for taking care of our climate just as we want to do with all aspects of Mother Nature, Planet Earth and our environment and ecology. This can be a very serious matter, as indicated in the major debates on climate change. It can also be a joyful one once we understand that everything is always changing and that we can do our part each day by being aware of the world in which we live. This awareness can begin at any time in our lives: as children we have a natural love of outdoors and play. Let us try to engage in this way throughout our days and years by sharing this in the spirit of play with our children and our children's children.

Climate Companions, friends and heroes is a developing story in which we can all participate in word, action and music. It is a second offering in which Eenie Meenie Beenie Bo has a special role as the reader will see!

I do hope that this can inspire your thoughts and raise your awareness and understanding of the wonderful world in which we live.

Dr. Linda Spedding

Educational Overview

THE CLIMATE AND THE WEATHER

"The greatest service you can give to the world is to take responsibility for yourself, your relationships and your environment." Prof. Dr. Svami Purna

When we talk about the climate, we usually mean the general conditions of the temperature: hot or cold, warm or cool, dry or humid, windy or calm. Scientists studying the prevailing typical weather conditions or patterns have found that our planet has experienced weather cycles and patterns over the centuries that have led to huge changes in habitation and impact how future generations may live. While we feel that we may not be able to make a big difference individually, we can affect the climate through our collective activities and even set individual examples for others to be encouraged by and perhaps follow. Climate campaigners, crusaders, champions and heroes are very much needed to comprehend the issues fully and to maintain a balanced approach to enable sound solutions and action in the face of any challenges in my humble opinion.

The first step is to understand, respect and honour the forces that are part of our climate. In this publication, I hope not only to raise awareness of the importance of the climate but also to increase reverence for the natural world so that we can protect our environment and sustain the best conditions for our children and our children's children. I have been passionate about energy and environmental issues during my career as an international environmental lawyer. I have considered this a vital interdisciplinary matter that should be part of our education as citizens of this Planet. Here, therefore, I am setting out a brief overview (as I understand and recall it) of the vast history and science of the climate below based upon published information I have reviewed over many years. This is to provide the setting for the verses that follow in this selection. A key message is to treat Mother Earth and the planetary forces with humility and love.

Climate study became part of military planning in the 1940s, during the Second World War and later at the outset of the Cold War, in order to understand the trajectory of fallout from a nuclear attack. Developments in long range weather forecasting as well as the launch of space programmes in the US and the Soviet Union provided further impetus and funding for climate science. The fear of sudden climate change began as a scare about global cooling during the 1960s moving to global warming in the 1980s. Former British Prime Minister Margaret Thatcher in the 1980s and Al Gore, as both a US Senator and later as Vice President in the 1990s, both pushed the climate change agenda at home and internationally. While a minor specialization for most of the last century, since the 1992

Earth Summit in Rio de Janeiro and the ratification of the Kyoto Treaty, climate study underpins every discipline. Collective action has become recognised as being paramount for our wellbeing. Indeed, many world leaders have come together in this regard: for instance President Obama has again very recently highlighted the significance of commitment to appropriate climate action globally.

I have often pointed out in my environmental work that the responsible players in this context are Government, Industry and the Public. Unfortunately, the engagement of scientists with politics and policy has sometimes led to a vicious circle which has generated more fear. For business climate change is a huge opportunity for profits in say, emissions trading, and reputational issues including public relations. The framework for action is generally driven by governments. This is why we individual inhabitants of the Earth should try to understand the position as far as possible and act responsibly as time evolves.

On the research front computer modelling is a tool for the understanding of climate mechanisms. However they are not proof: they are just projections of a hot future, based on an uncertain science. The more responsible approach is to live in a balanced and responsible manner, allowing the Earth to breathe in its natural breathing places and to respect the environment.

Greenhouse Gases and the Temperature

Instrumental measurements of Earth temperatures began only in the 1860s giving us nearly 150 years of information of varying quality. Most of this information is concentrated in the industrialised countries of the northern hemisphere, partly due to historical reasons of economic development, but mostly because some 80% of the southern hemisphere is ocean. The Earth's average temperature is 15 degrees Celsius due in part to the greenhouse effect. Certain gases, such as water vapour, carbon dioxide, methane, nitrous oxides, chlorofluorocarbons and ozone - trap a proportion of the Sun's heat within the atmosphere. These gases have become known as greenhouse gases. The relative proportion of trapped heat to that which is transported by air currents away from the Earth has been the subject of dispute for some time.

Scientists have debated changes in the climate and the weather for many years. Different opinions are supported by various evidence and case studies. For instance, some scientists believe that if humans do not curb "greenhouse gas" emissions, Earth temperatures will rise uncontrollably, melt ice sheets and cause huge sea level rises, as well as increase the frequency and strength of extreme events such as hurricanes. The Intergovernmental Panel on Climate Change (IPCC), created in 1988 by the United Nations and the World Meteorological Organisation (WMO), projects that global temperatures will rise between 1.4 and 5.8 degrees Celsius in the next century and concludes that human activity is responsible for warming the earth.

Apparently, there is still no overall complete agreement about the principal driving force for climate: whether it is the Sun, the Moon, plate tectonics, the carbon cycle, or indeed humanity. Indeed there is no certain prognosis about the likely upcoming climate and the impact on life on Earth although opinion is becoming less diverse. There is agreement on the following historic facts:

* That global mean temperatures have risen about 0.6 degrees Celsius over the past century.; and
* That concentration of carbon dioxide in the atmosphere has increased by about 30% since the industrial revolution.

Whereas there is no complete consensus about the role of increased levels in terms of temperature and carbon dioxide or its effect on the future climate, proactive steps are being taken through reports, meetings and debates about steps governments should implement in a responsible way. This may be seen as implementing the precautionary principle so that Earth's peoples collectively become responsible to mitigate any risks to our future climate.

Climate Causes

The climate we experience is the result of interactions among the oceans, the atmosphere, land and ice masses and the biosphere as the Earth spins on its own axis, is orbited by the Moon, and itself orbits the Sun. Some believe that the climate one day will shift into a catastrophic state. Others say that even if carbon dioxide concentrations were to triple, there would be little effect.

The Carbon Cycle

The situation is complicated by the blurring between what has happened as a result of human activity and what may be the result of a natural climate cycle. It has become clear that deforestation and subsequent soil erosion has limited the absorption of carbon dioxide. There is an overall recognised effect known as the carbon cycle by which carbon flows between the atmosphere, soil and vegetation, and to a lesser extent the oceans, then the Earth's crust, to be later found in volcanism or weathering back into the atmosphere. Volcanoes are known, in turn, to affect the climate patters. Their impact – and that of Plate Tectonics – has also been considered for some time, along with interactions between the atmosphere and the oceans.

The Sun

The Sun – and solar impact - is important to grasp from the outset. In Space the Earth is surrounded by the magnetosphere, which deflects high energy particles emitted by the Sun known as the solar wind, and which otherwise would burn the planet. About half of the solar energy, which impacts the Earth, is converted into heat on the Earth's surface. Sunspot activity, an upwelling of visible dark spots on the surface of the Sun, has some influence on climate. Changes in the Earth's orbit around the Sun, as well as the Earth's movement on its own axis have been explored as determinants of climate... Scientists also study the Moon to see changes in the fraction of sunlight that is reflected back into space.

Clouds

Clouds play an enormous part in the climate but are not well understood. They reflect the sun's radiation but there is also a coupling between surface temperatures and clouds. When the temperature changes the clouds change, and that in turn may amplify or diminish the temperature. This is known as "cloud feedback". No climate models have managed to simulate this effect.

Closing Remarks

Many have tried to forecast the climate and weather trends, setting out complicated and contradictory results. The resulting data sets are used in computational modelling to make correlations between say, global temperature and carbon dioxide concentrations, or sunspot activity with pressure anomalies, and most recently, sea surface temperatures and hurricane strengths. The trend is in favour of some agreement over rising temperatures on the Earth. However, academic literature has often warned that such correlations are not causality and of course many inexplicable and unexpected events occur that people cannot find answers to.

Climate extremes, such as hurricanes, are a normal part of climate processes, just as earthquakes are a normal part of Earth processes. They are not actually dangerous in themselves. They are dangerous because humans choose to live in their path. The strength of Hurricane Katrina was equivalent to about 12 Hiroshima bombs. The strength of the earthquake which caused the Asian tsunami was equivalent to 700 million Hiroshima bombs. These are forces human beings cannot combat, thus we need to understand and live with the different forces of nature and co-exist in a responsible, caring and positive way.

All of this rather complicated background has led to my creating a second in the adventure of Eenie Meenie Beenie Bo entitled Climate Companions (Heroes and Friends) in the hope to inspire as many as are ready to be a part of this ongoing story and live and learn and serve the environment and climate in a harmonious, joyful and peaceful manner.

Have you heard of Hotty?
Hotty rules the World
Hotty holds the victory card
At bad his power is hurled

Hotty watches over life
Hotty crushes pain and strife
Hotty cares for plants, trees, each flower
Please observe his positive power

Heat and dust may have their place
But why always live in arid space?
Water, greens, environment should flourish – all
When Hotty rules from his heavenly hall

Hotty comes at times of need
To show the value of any good deed
Hotty holds invisible strength to share
You can find him everywhere

So do not live in despair
Always live with hope
Face all challenge and pain
Hotty will bring healing rain

Let us now smile and sing – and
Let us Hotty energy bring
In ourselves and others to share
Always - for all - and those in our care

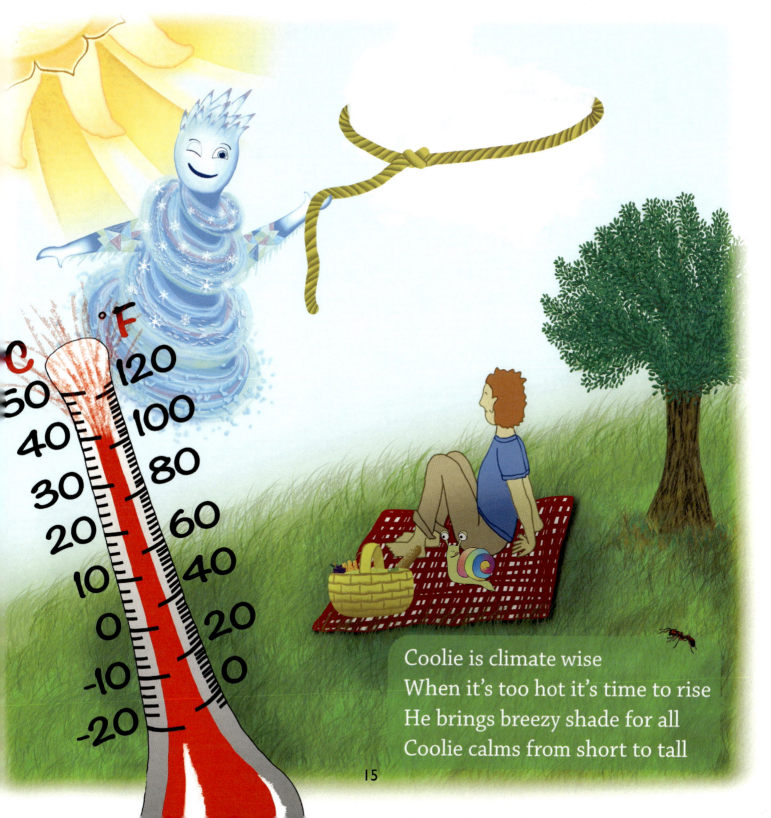

Coolie is climate wise
When it's too hot it's time to rise
He brings breezy shade for all
Coolie calms from short to tall

He loves to bring the rain and snow
And lets the weather balance show

Mrs. Moderate manages the weather scales
In climate patterns she never fails
Checking that the seasons flow
Respecting the elements you know

Mrs. Moderate comes at day or night
She brings her special smile and light
Her gentle touch is invisible to most
She is the guest of the enlightened host

Do you know the ways of Lord Sun?
The leader of the weather and climate
Without him all would be in the shade
And life in Earth would indeed fade

Let us to the climate be kind
And to nature be gentle and wise
Let us keep our weather and planet in mind
So that selfish habits may not arise

Have you heard of Dr. Wind?
Who blows whenever there is need

Who sends the soothing breeze
And stirs the air even in times of freeze

Often Dr. Wind with Mrs. Moderate work
Together and in tandem...
To balance the heat and cold
Even when this may seem random

At times more strength may manifest
In a gale, hurricane, typhoon, tempest
Followed by a quiet mood
That lets the crops emerge for our food

Have you heard of Master Rain?
Across the world he washes away pain
Letting all life enjoy a soothing sound
So that Mother Earth can with joy abound

Let us observe this natural splendour
Through the music that we render
Whether at work or at play
In harmony we can enjoy our day

Please remember Master Rain
To whom many sing while others complain
He serves with his climate friends
And brings relief to serve our ends

His cooling compassion clears the heat
Yet his warm effect has a wonderful beat
His sound can make us dance and sing
And crops and flowers also bring

Have you heard of the Voice of Time?
Who governs all in this rhyme
And teaches the value of all in life
To learn and grow with joy, not strife

When sun and rain are together bright
A rainbow shows its special light
An arc of beauty filled with love
A message from all who work above

Have you seen the wonders of the Rainbow
Who joins our weather patterns across the sky?
Shifting our emotions and bringing such wonder
Enabling the glory of life to glow from on high

ALL AROUND

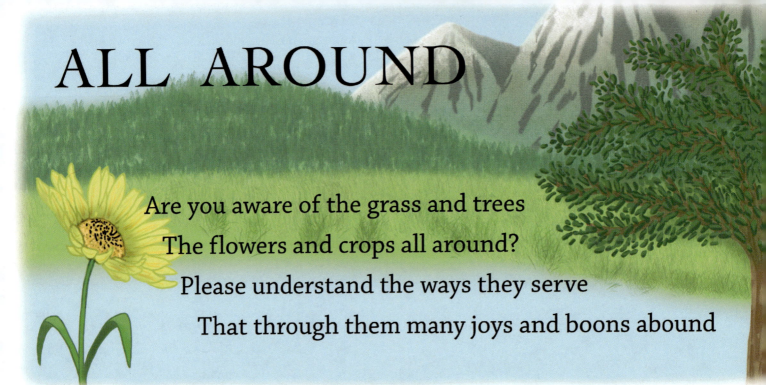

Are you aware of the grass and trees
The flowers and crops all around?
Please understand the ways they serve
That through them many joys and boons abound

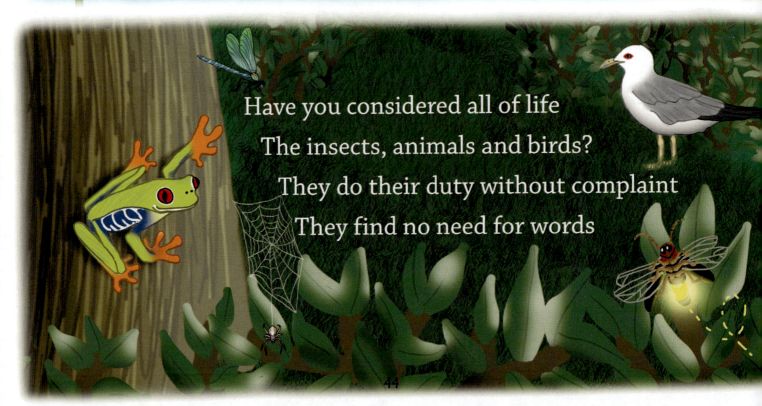

Have you considered all of life
The insects, animals and birds?
They do their duty without complaint
They find no need for words

Let us enjoy the way life flows
Let us be kind to our wonderful world
Let us all of nature conserve
And our gentle human spirit be unfurled

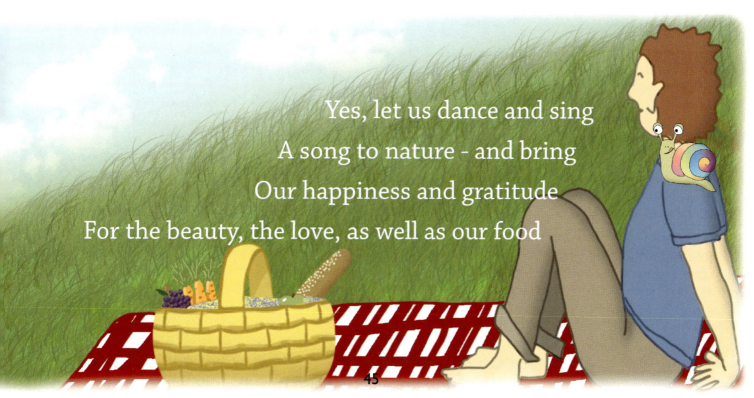

Yes, let us dance and sing
A song to nature - and bring
Our happiness and gratitude
For the beauty, the love, as well as our food

For additional information, other works from the author, accompanying music and games to the Eenie series of books and continuing education, please visit our website eeniemeeniebeeniebo.org

Made in the USA
Columbia, SC
18 November 2021